Ankita Rossi

Via Claudia Augusta Radweg
(Via Claudia Augusta Cycle Path)

Title: Via Claudia Augusta Radweg (Via Claudia Augusta Cycle Path)
Author: Ankita Rossi
Published by: NEXTUNICORN PUBLISHER PROPRIETORSHIP
Publisher's Address: Shree Dwarkadhish Ji Ka Was, Emri, Rajsamand, RAJASTHAN, India. Pincode: 313342
Printer Details: Published online on various platforms.
Edition: 01
ISBN: 978-81-968306-2-5

Images Source: Pixbay: (https://pixabay.com/)
All images' rights belong to their respective owners.
Disclaimer: The author and publisher disclaim all liability for accuracy, loss, or damage arising from the use of this travel guide; users are urged to independently verify information and prioritize personal safety.

Catalog

Discovering Historical Marvels

Embark on a journey through the Via Claudia Augusta Radweg and uncover a tapestry of history woven into its breathtaking landscapes. While Paris may boast its own charm, this route is adorned with cultural treasures, including enchanting towns like Füssen, Augsburg, and Trento. With a rich historical background, the Via Claudia Augusta Radweg unveils stories of ancient civilizations and medieval wonders, showcasing an enthralling blend of art and heritage.

Füssen: Where Fairytales Come to Life

Begin your adventure in Füssen, a town that exudes a fairytale ambiance. The Hohes Schloss (High Castle) and St. Mang's Abbey offer glimpses of medieval grandeur, setting the stage for the captivating journey ahead. Wander through cobbled streets, immerse yourself in local traditions, and discover hidden artistic nuances tucked away in this charming Bavarian enclave.

Augsburg: A Renaissance Dream

Known as the "Renaissance City," Augsburg echoes with echoes of history at every step. Marvel at the Augsburg Cathedral and Perlach Tower, which stand as testaments to bygone eras. The Fuggerei, recognized as the world's oldest social housing complex, serves as a living reminder of Augsburg's commitment to preserving both history and humanity.

Trento: Gateway to Alpine Majesty

As you venture further along the route, Trento reveals itself as a gateway to Alpine splendor. The Buonconsiglio Castle and Cathedral of Saint Vigilius transport you back in time while showcasing the cultural richness that has shaped this crossroads of civilizations. The Via Claudia Augusta Radweg seamlessly integrates these historical treasures into its scenic tapestry.

Unveiling Hidden Cultural Gems

Beyond well-known stops lie lesser-explored cultural wonders beckoning along the Via Claudia Augusta Radweg. Discover the medieval charm of Glorenza, admire the frescoes of San Silvestro in Aquiléia, or marvel at the ancient Amphitheatre in Augsburg. These hidden gems eagerly await your exploration along this historic route.

Embrace the Journey

The Via Claudia Augusta Radweg is more than just a path; it's a transformative journey through landscapes that resonate with tales of yore. As you traverse charming villages and picturesque valleys, take a moment to immerse yourself in the local way of life. Engage with artistic expressions, savor regional flavors, and relish in the simplicity that makes this journey truly unforgettable.

Culinary Delights

Indulge in culinary treasures scattered along the Via Claudia Augusta Radweg. From hearty Bavarian specialties in Füssen to Alpine-inspired dishes in Trento, each meal is a revelation. Sample local delicacies, immerse yourself in regional gastronomic heritage, and savor the flavors that define each stop along your way.

Breathtaking Scenery

The allure of the Via Claudia Augusta Radweg extends beyond cultural riches to embrace diverse natural landscapes. From Alpine foothills to picturesque banks of the River Adige, every segment of this route unveils a new chapter in nature's grandeur. Whether cycling through vineyard-covered hills or strolling along serene lakeshores, you will be captivated by landscapes as diverse as the historical tapestry it weaves.

Embark on an unforgettable journey along the Via Claudia Augusta Radweg where each pedal stroke propels you into a captivating blend of history, culture, and natural splendor. This isn't just a mere trip; it's an immersive experience delving into Europe's rich heritage at its core.

1. Füssen, Germany: A Fairytale Beginning

Füssen is a town with a fascinating medieval history, and one of its notable landmarks is the Hohes Schloss, also known as the High Castle. This castle serves as a testament to the town's past and offers visitors a chance to immerse themselves in its medieval charm.

If you're planning a visit, it's best to come during the spring or summer when the weather is pleasant and perfect for outdoor activities. The Hohes Schloss usually opens its doors at 10 AM and closes at 5 PM, giving you ample time to explore.

For more information or if you have any inquiries, you can reach out to them at +49 8362 903660. You can also visit their official website for additional details (https://www.hoheschloss-fuessen.de/en/).

Augsburg, known for its rich Renaissance history, boasts iconic landmarks such as Augsburg Cathedral and the Fuggerei, both of which have stood the test of time for centuries. If you're looking for a key attraction, make sure to explore Augsburg Cathedral and immerse yourself in the historical significance of the Fuggerei, which happens to be the world's oldest social housing complex. To make the most of your visit, it's recommended to plan your trip during late spring or early autumn when the weather is pleasant. Augsburg Cathedral typically opens its doors from 9 AM to 6 PM, allowing visitors ample time to soak in its architectural beauty. For any inquiries or further information, you can reach out via telephone at +49 821 3166 or visit their official website at [Official Website](https://www.augsburger-dom.de/).

3. Trento, Italy: Gateway to Alpine Majesty

Trento, a city that holds great historical importance in Italy, serves as the gateway to the majestic Alps. It is a place where perplexity and burstiness are intertwined. When you visit Trento, make sure to explore the remarkable Buonconsiglio Castle and marvel at the beauty of the Cathedral of Saint Vigilius. The summer months offer the perfect opportunity to immerse yourself in the breathtaking Alpine surroundings. If you plan on visiting Buonconsiglio Castle, note that it typically opens its doors from 10 AM to 6 PM. For any further information or inquiries, you can reach them at +39 0461 233770 or visit their official website at [Official Website](https://www.buonconsiglio.it/).

Glorenza, a medieval treasure, is known for its well-preserved architecture that reflects its rich historical importance. One of the key attractions is taking a leisurely walk through the enchanting medieval streets and marveling at the town's remarkable architecture. To avoid large crowds, it is recommended to plan your visit during late spring or early autumn. A hidden gem not to be missed are the medieval city walls, which provide breathtaking views of the surroundings. And when it comes to culinary delights, make sure to indulge in the local specialties at Gasthof zum Hirschen.

Bolzano, a city that combines the influences of Italy and Austria, has a rich history that dates back to Roman times. It offers a unique blend of culture and heritage. One of its key attractions is the Ötzi Museum, where you can immerse yourself in alpine elegance and learn about the fascinating history of the region. Additionally, Bolzano is known for its beautiful vineyards, which provide breathtaking views and an opportunity to indulge in the fall harvest season. If you're planning a visit, you can reach out to them at +39 0471 307000 or visit their official website for more information: [Official Website](https://www.museion.it/).

Verona, a city renowned for its rich Roman history and its connection to Shakespeare's timeless tale of Romeo and Juliet, offers a captivating blend of the past and the present. When visiting this enchanting destination, be sure to delve into the wonders of the Arena di Verona, an ancient amphitheater that stands as a testament to the city's historical significance. Additionally, take a stroll through the historic Piazza delle Erbe, where you can immerse yourself in the vibrant atmosphere of this bustling square. To make the most of your experience in Verona, plan your trip during the summer months when you can witness the world-famous opera season that beautifully unfolds within these ancient walls. If you need any further information or assistance, feel free to reach out via telephone at +39 045 800 5151 or visit our [Official Website](https://www.arena.it/).

Donauwörth, a delightful town situated at the meeting point of the Danube and Wörnitz rivers, holds a rich historical significance that can be traced back to the Middle Ages. Its captivating charm lies in its picturesque streets and the grandeur of Reichsstrasse, which are key attractions for visitors. For an optimal experience, late spring and early summer provide pleasant weather conditions to explore this beautiful town. And as a hidden gem, make sure not to overlook the Käthe-Kruse Doll Museum, which offers a unique and captivating experience.

Vipiteno, with its historic tower, is a true testament to its medieval past and importance as a bustling trade route. The town center and the Tower of the Twelve are the main attractions that exude an enchanting alpine charm. If you plan to visit, summer is the ideal time to explore the vibrant and colorful streets. For more information, you can contact them at +39 0472 767 600 or visit their [Official Website](https://www.sterzing.eu/).

9. Lienz, Austria: Mountain Majesty

Lienz, a place with a fascinating history that can be traced back to Roman times, is nestled amidst the breathtaking beauty of the Hohe Tauern National Park. One of its main attractions is the awe-inspiring Lienzer Dolomiten, where you can immerse yourself in the grandeur of the mountains. Additionally, the town square exudes a charming ambiance that is worth experiencing. For those planning a visit, it is recommended to come during the summer and early autumn seasons when the weather is pleasant and perfect for outdoor activities. As you explore this hidden gem, don't miss out on visiting Bruck Castle, which offers panoramic views that will leave you in awe.

Aichach, a charming town nestled by the Paar River, has a rich history that dates back to medieval times. Its picturesque setting makes it an ideal destination for those seeking tranquility by the riverside and an opportunity to delve into the historic Old Town. The best time to visit is during late spring or early summer when the weather is pleasant. Don't miss out on exploring the hidden gem of Schloss Blumenthal, renowned for its stunning gardens.

11. Venzone, Italy: Medieval Resilience

Venzone, a town with a remarkable history, has managed to rebuild itself after a catastrophic earthquake, displaying the unwavering strength of its medieval roots. Delve into the enchanting world of well-preserved medieval architecture and discover the town's distinctive layout. For an optimal experience, plan your visit during the vibrant seasons of spring and summer when you can fully immerse yourself in the reconstructed beauty.

Indulge in a culinary delight by savoring the local prosciutto at Antica Osteria Al Palazzo.

12. Schwaz, Austria: Mining Heritage

Schwaz has a rich history in mining and was a prominent hub for silver mining back in the Renaissance era. One of the main attractions is the Silver Mine, where you can immerse yourself in the fascinating mining heritage. Exploring the historic Old Town is also a must-do to get a glimpse into the past. If you plan to visit, summer is an ideal time as it offers guided tours of the Silver Mine. Additionally, don't miss out on visiting St. Mary's Chapel, which stands out with its magnificent Gothic architecture - truly a hidden gem worth exploring.

Regensburg's Old Town, which is recognized by UNESCO, is a remarkable reflection of its rich medieval and Roman past, situated along the beautiful Danube River. A key highlight of this historic area is the opportunity to meander through the enchanting Old Town and pay a visit to the iconic Stone Bridge. To make the most of your experience, it is recommended to plan your visit during late spring or early summer when the weather is pleasant for exploration. If you need any further information or wish to reach out, you can contact them at +49 941 5074410 or visit their [Official Website](https://www.regensburg.de/).

14. Toblach, Italy: Dolomite Delights

Toblach, nestled amidst the breathtaking Dolomite peaks, provides a picturesque getaway. One of its main attractions is the captivating Lake Toblach, which allows visitors to immerse themselves in the beauty of the Dolomites. The ideal time to visit this charming destination is during summer and early autumn, as it offers optimal conditions for hiking and enjoying outdoor activities. Additionally, a hidden gem worth exploring is the Gustav Mahler Composing Cottage, where you can delve into the rich musical history of Toblach.

Landsberg am Lech is a fascinating place steeped in history, showcasing its medieval beauty with intact town walls and a delightful old town. One of the main highlights is taking a stroll through its cobblestone streets and exploring the Hauptplatz. To make the most of your visit, late spring and early summer are ideal as the weather is pleasant and perfect for exploration. And when it comes to culinary delights, don't miss out on trying the local Leberkäse at an authentic Bavarian eatery.

Dornbirn is a lively cultural center with a modern architectural landscape and a thriving cultural scene. It offers a wide range of attractions for visitors to enjoy. One key attraction is the Inatura museum, where you can immerse yourself in the vibrant cultural scene of the city. Another must-visit spot is the Karren mountain, which offers breathtaking views and endless opportunities for exploration.

The great thing about Dornbirn is that it's appealing at any time of the year, thanks to its year-round cultural events. No matter when you decide to visit, you can always expect something exciting happening in this vibrant city.

If you need any information or have any questions, feel free to reach out via telephone at +43 5572 3060. You can also find more details on the official website: [Official Website](https://www.dornbirn.info/).

Bardolino, situated on the beautiful shores of Lake Garda, is renowned for its rich history and picturesque lakeside ambiance. One of its main attractions is the enchanting old town, which exudes a sense of charm and heritage. Additionally, visitors can indulge in the serene bliss of the lakeside, explore the fascinating Scaliger Castle, and take leisurely walks along the Lungolago promenade.

For those planning a visit, summer is an ideal time to fully immerse oneself in the vibrant lakeside atmosphere that Bardolino has to offer. The warm weather and pleasant surroundings create a perfect setting for relaxation and exploration.

If you need any further information or wish to get in touch with Bardolino's tourism office, you can reach them at +39 045 721 0071. Alternatively, you can visit their official website at https://www.bardolino.org/.

Augsburg's beer gardens have a rich history that spans centuries, deeply ingrained in its cultural fabric as a symbol of Bavarian hospitality. These establishments offer visitors an authentic experience of true Bavarian hospitality, immersing them in the traditional atmosphere of beer gardens. For those planning a visit, the summer season is particularly enticing, as beer gardens are at their peak popularity during this time, especially when beer festivals are taking place. In addition to the convivial ambiance, these beer gardens also tantalize taste buds with an array of culinary delights. Indulge in the flavors of traditional Bavarian dishes such as pretzels and sausages, perfectly complemented by regional beers that showcase the local brewing expertise.

Essential Tips for Your Via Claudia Augusta Radweg Adventure

Currency:
- The official currency used along the Via Claudia Augusta Radweg is the Euro (€).

Language:
- German is the primary language spoken along the Via Claudia Augusta Radweg. While English is commonly spoken in tourist areas, especially among younger locals, it can enhance your travel experience to learn a few basic German phrases and interact with residents.

Emergency Numbers:
- In case of emergencies, it's important to know these crucial contact numbers:
  - Ambulance: 112
  - Police: 110
  - Fire Department: 112
- If you're calling from outside the region, remember to dial your international access code first, followed by the country code (%49 for Germany and %43 for Austria), and then the number.

Useful Websites:
- Make the most of your experience with these helpful online resources:
  - Via Claudia Augusta Radweg Official Site: Explore detailed information about the route and get updates.
  - Deutsche Bahn (www.bahn.com): The official website of German railways for train travel information.
  - ÖBB (www.oebb.at): Austrian Federal Railways website for details on Austrian travel.
  - Alpine Pearls (www.alpine-pearls.com): Discover eco-friendly accommodations and activities along the route.

Daily Costs:
- Plan your budget accordingly with these estimated daily costs along the Via Claudia Augusta Radweg:
  - Budget (Less than €80): Affordable options including hostels, local eateries, and budget-friendly activities.

  - Midrange (€80–€150): Enjoy more comfort with midrange accommodations and a diverse range of dining experiences.
  - Top End (More than €150): Indulge in luxury accommodations, fine dining, and premium experiences.

Opening Hours:
- Operating hours may vary depending on the season:
  - Banks: Generally open from 9 AM to 5 PM, Monday to Friday.
  - Restaurants: Commonly open for lunch (noon–2 PM) and dinner (7 PM–10 PM).
  - Attractions: Check specific sites for seasonal opening hours.

Arriving on the Via Claudia Augusta Radweg:
- The arrival options may differ based on your starting point:
  - Munich Airport: Choose a direct train to your starting point or arrange a shuttle service.
  - Innsbruck Airport: Convenient train services are available for a smooth transition to your cycling adventure.
  - Verona Airport: Explore train options or arrange for a local transfer service for a comfortable arrival.
  - Venice Marco Polo Airport: Access the route via train or arrange a transfer for a relaxed start to your journey.

With these practical tips in mind, embark on your Via Claudia Augusta Radweg adventure well-prepared for a seamless and enriching exploration of the route's cultural, historical, and natural wonders.

Danube to the Adriatic - 2 Weeks

Embark on an extraordinary cycling journey along the Via Claudia Augusta Radweg, spanning from the Danube to the Adriatic Sea. Get ready for a captivating adventure filled with diverse landscapes and cultural experiences.

Day 1 - 3: Donauwörth, Germany

Start your adventure in Donauwörth, a charming town located at the confluence of the Danube and Wörnitz rivers. Take your time exploring its picturesque streets and immerse yourself in the delightful riverside ambiance.

Day 4 - 6: Augsburg, Germany

Continue your cycling expedition to Augsburg, a city steeped in Renaissance history. Stroll through its captivating streets adorned with beautiful porticos, visit Augsburg Cathedral, and treat yourself to the local cuisine that reflects its rich cultural heritage.

Day 7 - 9: Trento, Italy

Crossing into Italy, you'll reach Trento, which serves as a gateway to the majestic Alps. Immerse yourself in the Alpine beauty as you visit landmarks like Buonconsiglio Castle and the Cathedral of Saint Vigilius.

Day 10 - 12: Bolzano, Italy

Keep pedaling towards Bolzano, surrounded by breathtaking alpine elegance. Explore fascinating attractions like the Ötzi Museum that showcases ancient artifacts and take in stunning mountain views while wandering through vineyards.

Day 13 - 15: Verona, Italy

Your final destination is Verona, known as the city of Shakespearean romance. Lose yourself in its historic Piazza delle Erbe, marvel at the grandeur of Arena di Verona, and soak up the enchanting atmosphere that permeates this captivating city.

Medieval Marvels - 2 Weeks

Embark on a thrilling cycling exploration through medieval marvels along the Via Claudia Augusta Radweg. Prepare to be transported back in time as you discover the rich history and architectural wonders of these hidden gems.

Day 1 - 3: Füssen, Germany

Begin your journey in Füssen, a town brimming with medieval charm and home to the iconic Hohes Schloss (High Castle). Immerse yourself in the fairytale-like atmosphere before setting off on your cycling adventure.

Day 4 - 6: Glorenza, Italy

Cycle into the enchanting medieval ambiance of Glorenza, a hidden gem boasting well-preserved architecture and a fascinating cultural heritage. Lose yourself in its narrow streets and soak up the historical charm.

Day 7 - 9: Venzone, Italy

Explore Venzone, a town that has risen from the ashes after a devastating earthquake. Marvel at its well-preserved medieval architecture and delve into its resilient history that showcases the strength of its people.

Day 10 - 12: Schwaz, Austria

Delve into Schwaz's rich mining heritage as you visit the iconic Silver Mine and explore its historic Old Town. Let yourself be captivated by the medieval charm embedded in every corner of this remarkable place.

Day 13 - 15: Landsberg am Lech, Germany

Conclude your journey in Landsberg am Lech, a true medieval gem with impeccably preserved town walls and charming cobblestone streets. Take a moment to reflect on all the mesmerizing medieval marvels you've encountered along your adventure on Via Claudia Augusta Radweg.

Culinary & Cultural Delights - 2 Weeks

Prepare to indulge your senses in an unforgettable culinary and cultural experience along the Via Claudia Augusta Radweg. Get ready for mouthwatering flavors and captivating cultural encounters.

Day 1 - 3: Vipiteno, Italy

Begin your gastronomic journey in Vipiteno, renowned for its alpine charm. Explore the town's historic towers, savor the local flavors that tantalize your taste buds, and immerse yourself in the vibrant town center.

Day 4 - 6: Aichach, Germany

Cycle to Aichach, a picturesque town nestled along the banks of the Paar River. Enjoy moments of riverside tranquility while indulging in regional culinary delights that showcase the authentic flavors of the area.

Day 7 - 9: Bardolino, Italy

Experience pure lakeside bliss in Bardolino, situated on the shores of a serene lake. Get lost in the charming old town's narrow streets, visit local wineries to sample delightful wines, and treat yourself to lakeside culinary offerings that will leave you craving for more.

Day 10 - 12: Dornbirn, Austria

Immerse yourself in the vibrant cultural hub of Dornbirn with its modern architecture, museums filled with artistic treasures, and lively events that showcase local talents. Take pleasure in exploring its diverse culinary scene and visiting cultural attractions that bring this city to life.

Day 13 - 15: Toblach, Italy

Conclude your culinary journey in Toblach surrounded by the majestic peaks of the Dolomites. Delight your senses with Dolomite-inspired dishes and savor every bite as you explore this breathtaking region known for its natural beauty and rich culinary traditions.

The Ancient Origins
The Via Claudia Augusta Radweg has a fascinating history that dates back to the time of the Roman Empire. It showcases the incredible engineering skills of ancient civilizations and the forward-thinking mindset of Roman rulers. Emperor Augustus initiated this project in 15 BCE, envisioning a crucial military road that would connect Altinum (modern-day Altino, Italy) on the Adriatic Sea to Donauwörth (Germany) on the Danube River. This strategic route was designed to enable swift movement of troops and supplies across different Roman provinces.
The construction of this road was an impressive feat of engineering. Stretching over 500 kilometers, it crossed various terrains, from the plains of the Po River to the Alpine foothills and beyond. Roman engineers employed advanced techniques such as stone-paved surfaces, bridges, and tunnels to overcome geographical challenges. The Via Claudia Augusta became a lifeline for the Roman military and played a significant role in promoting trade, cultural exchange, and economic development along its path.
Renaissance and Rediscovery
As time passed and the Roman Empire declined, so did the importance of the Via Claudia Augusta. However, during the Renaissance period, there was a renewed interest in classical antiquity which led to a rediscovery of ancient Roman roads. In the 16th century, scholars and travelers began documenting these forgotten routes once again. The Via Claudia Augusta captured their imagination and became an object of fascination for historians and explorers alike.
Recognizing its historical value as well as its economic potential, Habsburg rulers took initiatives to revive this ancient road in the 16th century. They undertook restoration efforts to upgrade it into a key trade route once again. This rejuvenation not only stimulated economic activities but also facilitated cultural

exchange as merchants, scholars, and artists traveled along this path contributing their unique stories to regional history.

Modern Revitalization

In recent times, there has been a growing interest in sustainable and recreational tourism. This led to the idea of transforming the ancient Via Claudia Augusta into a modern cycling route. The European Union and regional authorities collaborated to develop the Via Claudia Augusta Radweg, aiming to preserve its historical significance while promoting eco-friendly travel and cross-cultural experiences.

The planning and development of this cycling route involved adapting the ancient path to modern standards. Infrastructure improvements, signage, and amenities were strategically implemented to ensure a seamless and enjoyable journey for cyclists. The revival of this route not only celebrates its historical roots but also opens up new opportunities for exploration, inviting enthusiasts to experience the same landscapes that once echoed with the footsteps of Roman legions.

Today's Cultural and Recreational Gem

Today, the Via Claudia Augusta Radweg stands as a living testament to ancient engineering brilliance and historical resilience. Spanning across three countries - Italy, Germany, and Austria - this cycling route encapsulates a captivating blend of history, culture, and natural beauty. Travelers embarking on this journey not only pedal through picturesque landscapes but also uncover stories embedded in the stones of ancient Roman roads.

The cultural and recreational significance of the Via Claudia Augusta Radweg continues to grow. Cyclists, historians, and adventure seekers from around the world embark on this unique journey that offers a harmonious coexistence between ancient wonders and modern experiences. What was once a military highway has transformed into a corridor of cultural exchange that connects diverse communities while inviting travelers to relive the history that shaped these regions.

In conclusion, the history of Via Claudia Augusta Radweg is an enthralling narrative that spans millennia. From its inception as an important Roman road to its revitalization during the Renaissance period and its modern transformation into a popular cycling route, it has evolved while still preserving its essence. Today, as both a cultural gem and recreational attraction, it welcomes all those who venture along its path to become part of its living history.

Accommodation Along the Via Claudia Augusta Radweg

Accommodation options along the Via Claudia Augusta Radweg are diverse and offer a unique and immersive experience for travelers. In this comprehensive guide, we will explore different types of lodgings that cater to various preferences and budgets.

1. Historic Inns and Gasthofs:
   - Price Range: €50 - €120 per night
   - Along the enchanting landscapes of the Via Claudia Augusta Radweg, cyclists can find historic inns and traditional gasthofs that provide a charming blend of comfort and cultural authenticity.
   - These accommodations have been meticulously restored, giving travelers a glimpse into the rich history of the region while offering modern amenities for their convenience.
   - Set against picturesque villages, these family-run inns ensure a warm and personalized stay.

2. Alpine Mountain Huts:
   - Price Range: €20 - €30 per person per night
   - Venturing into the Alpine stretches of the route, cyclists may come across mountain huts or rifugi nestled in breathtaking peaks. These huts offer a unique mountain retreat.
   - Accommodations range from shared dormitories to private double rooms, providing a cozy haven for those seeking an immersive mountain experience.
   - Due to limited availability, it is essential to book in advance. Many of these rustic refuges are managed by the Club Alpino Italiano (CAI).

3. Countryside Agriturismi:
   - Price Range: €60 - €150 per night
   - The tranquil countryside along the Via Claudia Augusta Radweg is adorned with agriturismi, farm stays that allow travelers to immerse themselves in rural life.
   - These accommodations offer an authentic taste of local culture and often feature organic produce, homemade delicacies, and opportunities to participate in farm activities.

- Cyclists can choose from rustic cottages to elegant farmhouses for an authentic and peaceful retreat.

4. Riverside Retreats:
   - Price Range: €70 - €200 per night
   - As the route winds along riverbanks, cyclists may discover charming riverside retreats that provide a serene atmosphere for relaxation.
   - With panoramic views of flowing waters and surrounding landscapes, these accommodations offer a peaceful respite after a day of cycling.
   - Some retreats also provide water-based activities, allowing travelers to further connect with the natural beauty along the route.

5. Historical Castles Turned Hotels:
   - Price Range: €80 - €250 per night
   - History and architecture enthusiasts can indulge in a unique experience by staying in historical castles turned hotels along the Via Claudia Augusta Radweg.
   - These accommodations seamlessly blend medieval charm with modern comfort, offering an unforgettable stay in rooms adorned with centuries-old character.
   - Cyclists can take a step back in time while enjoying luxurious amenities within the walls of these storied structures.

6. Chic Urban Boutique Hotels:
   - Price Range: €100 - €300 per night
   - Urban stretches of the route, particularly those passing through vibrant cities, present opportunities to stay in chic boutique hotels.
   - These modern and stylish accommodations cater to urban travelers, providing a sophisticated stay with proximity to cultural attractions, dining options, and entertainment venues.
   - Cyclists can enjoy the convenience of city life without compromising on comfort and elegance.

7. Cycling-Focused Hostels:
   - Price Range: €30 - €60 per night
   - In recognition of the growing popularity of cycling tourism, there are hostels designed especially for cyclists.

- These hostels provide secure bike storage, repair facilities, and valuable insights into the best cycling routes and attractions in the area.
   - Travelers can connect with like-minded cyclists and share their experiences in these specialized accommodations.
8. Scenic Lakeside Retreats:
   - Price Range: €80 - €180 per night
   - Along the picturesque lakes on the Via Claudia Augusta Radweg, you can find serene lakeside retreats that offer a tranquil escape.
   - With stunning views of the water and surrounding landscapes, these accommodations provide a peaceful ambiance for unwinding after a day of cycling.
   - Travelers can also enjoy local lakeside activities and savor the serenity of these idyllic retreats.
9. Breathtaking Mountain Chalets:
   - Price Range: €70 - €200 per night
   - For those seeking an intimate lodging option while traversing mountainous terrains, mountain chalets are perfect.
   - Surrounded by the grandeur of the Alps, these chalets offer cozy interiors, fireplaces, and panoramic views.
   - Cyclists can experience the magic of mountains while enjoying all the comforts provided by these alpine retreats.
10. Modern Riverside Hotels:
   - Price Range: €90-€250 per night
   — Along riverfront stretches of the route, you'll find modern riverside hotels that offer contemporary accommodations with stunning water views.
   — Cyclists can enjoy modern amenities, riverside dining, and easy access to the scenic beauty of the surrounding landscapes.
   — These hotels provide a perfect blend of comfort and natural splendor.

Embarking on the journey along the Via Claudia Augusta Radweg involves understanding the complexities of visa and residency regulations. Here is a comprehensive guide to help travelers navigate this historic route with ease:

1. Schengen Treaty for European Citizens:

- European citizens from countries within the Schengen Treaty can enter Italy effortlessly by presenting a valid identity card or passport.

2. Visa Exemptions for Select Countries:

- Travelers from 28 non-EU nations, including Australia, Brazil, Canada, Israel, Japan, New Zealand, and the USA, are exempted from visas for tourist visits up to 90 days. It's important to note that visa requirements may vary for those planning to travel to the UK and Ireland.

3. Visas for Non-EU and Non-Schengen Nationals:

- Non-EU and non-Schengen nationals who intend to stay in Italy for more than 90 days or have purposes other than tourism, such as work or study, may need specific visas.

- For accurate and up-to-date visa information, it is recommended to refer to the official website www.esteri.it/visti/home_eng.asp or contact an Italian consulate.

4. Residence and Work for EU Citizens:

- EU citizens have the privilege of living and working in Italy without permits. However, those staying longer than three months must register at the municipal registry office and provide evidence of employment or sufficient financial resources.

5. Permanent Residence for Non-EU Foreign Citizens:

- Non-EU foreign citizens who have legally resided in Italy uninterrupted for five years can apply for permanent residence status.

6. Permesso di Soggiorno (Permit to Stay):

- Non-EU citizens planning to stay at a single address for more than one week must obtain a 'permesso di soggiorno' from the local police station.

- Tourists staying in hotels are generally exempt from this requirement.

- The application process for a 'permesso di soggiorno' is necessary for studying, working, or extended residence. EU citizens are exempt from this requirement.

7. Study Visas:

- Non-EU citizens who wish to study at Italian universities or language schools should apply for a study visa at the nearest Italian embassy or consulate.

- Essential documents include proof of enrollment, fee payments, and sufficient financial means.

- Study visas align with the duration of enrollment and can be renewed in Italy based on ongoing enrollment and financial stability.

Understanding these visa and residency nuances is essential for a smooth and compliant journey along the Via Claudia Augusta Radweg. As regulations may change over time, staying updated through official channels ensures a hassle-free exploration of this historic route.

Embarking on the Via Claudia Augusta Radweg is like embarking on a captivating journey through diverse landscapes. Each season unveils its own unique charm, making it an enchanting experience for cycling enthusiasts. From the vibrant bloom of spring to the sun-soaked days of summer, from the rich hues of autumn to the serene tranquility of winter, there's something special waiting for every traveler along this route.

1. Spring Awakening (April - June):

- As winter gives way to spring, the Via Claudia Augusta Radweg comes alive with bursts of color. In April, wildflowers line the route, creating a picturesque tapestry of colors that is truly breathtaking.

- The mild temperatures during spring provide an ideal climate for cycling. It's a time when riders can enjoy nature awakening without having to endure the intense heat of summer.

- Charming towns along the route also come alive during this season, hosting local festivals that celebrate both nature's bounty and cultural heritage.

2. Summer Splendor (July - August):

- Summer bathes the Via Claudia Augusta Radweg in radiant sunshine, painting a golden glow over its scenic landscapes. The vibrant greenery and clear skies create a postcard-perfect backdrop for cyclists.

- The warm temperatures invite travelers to explore historical treasures and indulge in local cuisine. Outdoor events and festivals add to the lively spirit of summer along the route.

3. Autumn Tapestry (September - October):

- As summer bids farewell, autumn unfolds along the route with its rich and warm hues. The changing foliage adds a touch of magic to the journey as reds, oranges, and yellows paint a beautiful tapestry.

- Cyclists who ride through Via Claudia Augusta Radweg during autumn are treated to milder temperatures, making it an ideal time for leisurely rides. Towns and vineyards celebrate grape harvests, offering a chance to enjoy local wines and festivities.

4. Winter Serenity (November - March):

- Winter brings a serene spell to the Via Claudia Augusta Radweg, turning it into a tranquil haven. Although cycling activity may slow down during this season, winter offers a unique allure for those seeking peace and reflection.

- The snow-capped peaks of the Alps create a breathtaking backdrop, and the historic towns along the route exude a quiet charm. Travelers can enjoy the cozy accommodations, warm hospitality, and occasional winter markets.

Each season along the Via Claudia Augusta Radweg offers its own distinct experience. It weaves together natural beauty, cultural richness, and historical significance into an unforgettable cycling adventure that can be enjoyed all year round. Whether you're under the blossoms of spring or basking in the warmth of summer, surrounded by vibrant autumn hues or embracing the peacefulness of winter, this route promises an incredible journey for every traveler.

Embark on a captivating adventure along the Via Claudia Augusta Radweg, where you'll be treated to an enchanting journey through scenic splendors. Let's explore the different sections of this incredible route:

Section 1: Donauwörth to Augsburg

Covering a distance of approximately 90 km, this section will take you through picturesque landscapes along the Danube River. Start your journey in Donauwörth and pedal your way to Augsburg, a city steeped in rich Roman history. Don't forget to explore the fascinating Fugger Houses and Augsburg Cathedral.

Section 2: Augsburg to Landsberg am Lech

With around 55 km to cover, this section will lead you through the charming Bavarian countryside, passing by quaint villages along the way. Your destination is Landsberg am Lech, renowned for its medieval Old Town and the picturesque River Lech.

Section 3: Landsberg am Lech to Füssen

Traverse approximately 65 km of lush landscapes as you make your way towards Füssen. Immerse yourself in the charm of this town as you discover its Hohes Schloss and wander through its enchanting streets. And don't miss out on visiting the breathtaking Neuschwanstein Castle.

Section 4: Füssen to Imst

Prepare for a scenic adventure covering about 90 km as you cycle through the Alpine region and cross into Austria. Imst awaits with its historic charm, and be sure not to miss the awe-inspiring natural wonder of Rosengartenschlucht Gorge.

Section 5: Imst to Landeck

Enjoy a delightful ride along the Inn River for approximately 45 km while being surrounded by majestic mountain vistas. Your destination is Landeck, known for its medieval castle that holds stories from times long past.

Section 6: Landeck to Nauders

Covering around 40 km, this section will take you through the captivating Tyrolean landscapes until you reach the charming town of Nauders. Along the way, be mesmerized by the Reschensee and its submerged church, a sight that will leave you in awe.

Section 7: Nauders to Merano/Meran

Prepare for an exciting border-crossing adventure into Italy as you descend into the South Tyrol region, covering about 70 km. Your journey will lead you to Merano/Meran, famous for its spa culture and stunning botanical gardens.

Section 8: Merano/Meran to Trento

Cycle through the Adige Valley for approximately 70 km, passing by vineyards and orchards along the way. Your ultimate destination is Trento, a city that boasts a captivating blend of medieval and Renaissance architecture.

Section 9: Trento to Verona

Set off on a picturesque journey covering around 100 km through the Veneto region. Pedal your way through charming villages until you reach Verona, known for its iconic Roman Arena and its connections to Shakespeare.

Section 10: Verona to Vicenza

Prepare yourself for an enchanting ride through the Italian countryside as you cover approximately 90 km towards Vicenza. This UNESCO World Heritage site is home to architectural treasures designed by Palladio that are sure to leave you in awe.

Section 11: Vicenza to Padua

With about 40 km ahead of you, cycle through the Venetian plains until you arrive in Padua. Explore this historic city center and make sure not to miss out on visiting the renowned Scrovegni Chapel.

Section 12: Padua to Venice

Conclude your unforgettable journey with a final leg of approximately 40 km that takes you from Padua all the way to Venice - an iconic city known for its enchanting canals. Immerse yourself in the beauty of St. Mark's Square, the Doge's Palace, and the winding streets of this unique destination.

Elevation Profiles and Difficulty Ratings

When it comes to the Via Claudia Augusta Radweg, cyclists can expect a diverse range of terrains and challenges. The route offers a mix of flat stretches along riverbanks, gradual ascents and descents in hilly areas, and even some tough climbs in the Alpine regions. This variety ensures that riders will have an exciting and engaging journey.

The difficulty ratings for the route span from easy to moderate, making it accessible to cyclists of all skill levels. Whether you're a beginner or an experienced rider, there are sections that will suit your abilities.

As cyclists navigate through the route, they will be treated to elevation profiles characterized by gentle slopes. These slopes not only make for a pleasant ride but also offer breathtaking panoramic views of the surrounding landscapes.

To make their experience even more tailored, cyclists have the option to customize their journey by selecting specific sections based on their preferences and skill levels. This flexibility ensures that each cyclist can have a fulfilling adventure along the Via Claudia Augusta Radweg.

Welcome to the world of Via Claudia Augusta Radweg, where cyclists embark on a breathtaking journey that not only offers scenic beauty but also immerses them in the vibrant local culture through a series of events and festivals. To help you plan your adventure and make the most of each region's unique festivities, here is a handpicked calendar that showcases the best events along the route throughout the year.

1. Spring Delights: March to May

- South Tyrolean Spring Festival (Südtiroler Frühlingsfest): Get ready to celebrate the arrival of spring in Merano/Meran with a lively festival filled with music, traditional dances, and mouthwatering local cuisine.

- Verona in Love (Verona in Amore): If you find yourself cycling through Verona in May, be prepared to be enchanted by its romantic atmosphere during "Verona in Love." Enjoy concerts, street performances, and events inspired by Shakespeare's timeless tales.

2. Summer Revelry: June to August

- Füssen Festival Weeks (Füssener Festwochen): Immerse yourself in the arts as Füssen hosts a series of concerts, theater performances, and cultural events throughout summer.

- Imst Alpine Festival (Imster Bergfest): Experience true Tyrolean culture as you soak up the festive ambiance of Imst's Alpine Festival. Traditional music, folk dances, and local delicacies will transport you to another world.

- Merano Music Weeks (Meraner Musikwochen): July brings classical music enthusiasts an opportunity to enjoy mesmerizing performances at enchanting venues during the Merano Music Weeks.

3. Autumn Harvest: September to November

- Törggelen in South Tyrol: As autumn paints its colors across South Tyrol, join the Törggelen tradition. Explore wine cellars, taste new wine (Suser), and savor regional specialties that will tantalize your taste buds.

- Vinitaly in Verona: Wine lovers passing through Verona in November can indulge in Vinitaly, one of the world's largest wine exhibitions. Get ready for tastings and a series of wine-related events that will leave you craving for more.

4. Winter Celebrations: December to February

- Christmas Markets in Trento and Verona: Immerse yourself in the magic of Italian Christmas markets as you visit Trento and Verona. Delight in festive decorations, local crafts, and seasonal treats that will warm your heart.

- Carnival in Venice: Conclude your unforgettable journey by arriving in Venice during February to witness the world-famous Carnival. Prepare to be amazed by elaborate masks, lively parades, and an atmosphere filled with joyous energy.

5. Year-Round Cultural Gems

- Augsburg Mozart Festival: Classical music enthusiasts visiting Augsburg in May can't miss the Augsburg Mozart Festival, where concerts dedicated to the musical genius await their eager ears.

- Landeck Knights' Tournament (Landecker Ritterspiele): History comes alive in Landeck with an annual medieval knights' tournament that showcases thrilling jousting matches, archery competitions, and traditional crafts.

- Verona Opera Festival: For opera aficionados, plan your journey to coincide with the Verona Opera Festival held at the iconic Arena di Verona during summer months for an unforgettable musical experience.

This thoughtfully curated events calendar ensures that cyclists along Via Claudia Augusta Radweg can fully immerse themselves in the rich cultural tapestry of each region they pass through. Whether it's music festivals, artistic performances, or traditional celebrations, each event adds a unique flavor to the historic cycling adventure that awaits you. So get ready to pedal your way into an unforgettable experience filled with captivating stories, vivid imagery, and a sense of genuine human connection.

Donauwörth, Germany: The Starting Point

The cycling adventure begins in the charming town of Donauwörth, situated in Germany. As you embark on this journey, make sure to explore the historic Old Town and the magnificent Schloss Mangoldstein. To start your route, follow the clearly marked signs that say "Via Claudia Augusta" and head south towards Augsburg.

Augsburg: Where History Meets Modernity

Upon reaching Augsburg, you'll be greeted by a city that seamlessly blends medieval charm with modern vibrancy. Take some time to marvel at the Augsburg Cathedral and visit the Fuggerei, which holds the distinction of being the world's oldest social housing complex. To continue your journey, simply follow the signs through Augsburg's city center as you make your way towards Landsberg am Lech.

Landsberg am Lech: Historic Beauty

Nestled along the picturesque Lech River is Landsberg am Lech, a town exuding historic beauty. Don't miss out on exploring Hauptplatz with its medieval architecture and taking in the grandeur of Landsberg Castle. As you continue your cycling adventure, follow the Via Claudia Augusta signs and head southeast while crossing over the Lech River.

Schongau: Gateway to the Alps

Schongau awaits with its well-preserved medieval town center as a warm welcome for cyclists like yourself. Take some time to soak in its history by exploring its city walls and visiting the Pilgrimage Church of St. Jacob. Your route will lead you southeast from here as you cross over another stretch of Lech River on your way to Peiting.

Peiting to Füssen: Alpine Majesty

As you approach Füssen, prepare yourself for breathtaking views of Alpine majesty that become more pronounced along this leg of your journey. Be sure to take a ride along Forggensee Lake and immerse yourself in the awe-inspiring scenery of the Alps. To continue, simply keep heading south until you reach Füssen, marking the end of the German portion of your adventure.

Reutte, Austria: Crossing Borders

As you enter Austria through Reutte, a town nestled in the Ausserfern region, be prepared to experience a change in scenery. Take some time to admire the Ehrenberg Castle Ensemble and cross the impressive Highline 179 suspension bridge. Your route will take you south through scenic Austrian landscapes as you make your way towards Nassereith.

Imst: Tyrolean Traditions

Imst offers a delightful taste of Tyrolean culture against a backdrop of stunning mountains. Make sure to visit the Starkenberg Brewery and explore the charming Old Town for an authentic experience. Continuing your journey southward, you'll traverse the Imster Schlucht gorge as you head towards Landeck.

Landeck: Historic Trading Hub

Situated on the banks of Inn River lies Landeck, a historic market town waiting to be explored. Don't miss out on visiting Schrofenstein Castle and St. Catherine's Church while you're here. To proceed further, follow the Inn River as it guides you southward towards Nauders.

Reschen Pass: Alpine Summit

Prepare yourself for an alpine adventure as you cross Reschen Pass, marking the border between Austria and Italy. Marvel at the sight of a submerged church tower in Lake Reschen along your way. Descending into Italy, your cycling route will take you through Graun before continuing southward towards Merano.

Merano: Mediterranean Flair

Welcome to Merano! This charming town is known for its spa culture and Mediterranean atmosphere that adds a touch of relaxation to your journey's end. Be sure to unwind at Merano Thermal Baths and take a leisurely stroll through Trauttmansdorff Castle gardens before concluding your captivating Via Claudia Augusta Radweg adventure. To complete your journey, head south to Bolzano.

Donauwörth, Germany: The Starting Point
When it comes to exploring Donauwörth, Germany, there are two hotels that you should consider. One of them is Hotel Am Triller, located at Zirgesheimer Str. 14, Donauwörth. You can reach them at +49 906 996160 or visit their website [Hotel Am Triller](https://www.hotel-am-triller.de/). Another option is Parkhotel Donauwörth situated at Pflegstrasse 42 in the same city. To make a reservation or inquire about their services, you can contact them at +49 906 70590 or check out their website [Parkhotel Donauwörth](https://www.parkhotel-donauwoerth.de/).

Augsburg: Where History Meets Modernity
In Augsburg, Germany, there are two hotels that perfectly blend history and modernity. Dorint An Der Kongresshalle Augsburg is located at Imhofstraße 12 and offers a unique experience. For bookings or more information, you can reach them at +49 821 59740 or visit their website [Dorint An Der Kongresshalle Augsburg](https://hotel-augsburg.dorint.com/en/). Another option is IntercityHotel Augsburg situated at Halderstraße 29. To make a reservation or learn more about their amenities, you can contact them at +49 821 56700 or explore their website [IntercityHotel Augsburg](https://www.intercityhotel.com/en/hotels/all-hotels/germany/augsburg/intercityhotel-augsburg).

Landsberg am Lech: Historic Beauty
If you want to immerse yourself in the historic beauty of Landsberg am Lech in Germany, there are two hotels worth considering. Hotel Goggl, located at Ludwigstraße 7, is a fantastic choice. For bookings or inquiries, you can reach them at +49 8191 3050 or visit their website [Hotel Goggl](https://www.hotelgoggl.com/). Another option is Hotel Gasthof Stift situated at Stadtplatz 2. To make a reservation or explore their services, you can contact them at +49 8191 98020 or

check out their website [Hotel Gasthof Stift](https://www.hotel-stift-landsberg.de/).

Schongau: Gateway to the Alps

In Schongau, Germany, which serves as the gateway to the Alps, there are two hotels that offer excellent accommodation options. Hotel Holl Garni is located at Herzog-Ernst-Straße 7 and provides a comfortable stay experience. To make a reservation or inquire about their services, you can contact them at +49 8861 30970 or visit their website [Hotel Holl Garni](https://www.hotel-holl.com/). Another option is Hotel Alte Post situated at Marienplatz 19 in Schongau. To book a room or learn more about their facilities, you can contact them at +49 8861 28740 or explore their website [Hotel Alte Post](https://www.altepost-schongau.de/).

In Peiting, Germany, we have the exquisite Hotel Welfen. Located at August-Landmesser-Str. 6, this hotel offers top-notch services and facilities. To make a reservation or learn more about Hotel Welfen, you can visit their website [here](https://www.hotel-welfen.de/) or give them a call at +49 8861 67310.

Another fantastic option in Schwangau, Germany is Hotel Ludwigs. Situated at Lauterbachstr. 8, this hotel guarantees a delightful experience during your stay. For bookings or further information about Hotel Ludwigs, feel free to check out their website [here](https://www.ludwigs.de/en/) or contact them at +49 8362 8120.

Now let's move on to Reutte, Austria - a place known for its picturesque landscapes and rich history. The first recommendation in Reutte is Hotel Zum Mohren located at Untermarkt 26. This charming hotel offers impeccable service and cozy accommodations for your enjoyment. To book a room or explore more about Hotel Zum Mohren, visit their website [here](https://www.zum-mohren.at/) or simply dial +43 5672 62276.

Hotel Goldener Hirsch situated at Klause 94 in Höfen, Austria. With its warm ambiance and excellent amenities, this hotel guarantees an unforgettable stay in Reutte. To make reservations or find out more about Hotel Goldener Hirsch, check out their website [here](https://www.hotel-hirsch.at/en/) or give them a call at +43 5672 62372.

Let's explore two captivating hotels in Imst, Austria.

First up is the renowned Hotel Auderer, located at Pfarrgasse 42, Imst, Austria. You can reach them at +43 5412 66377 or visit their website [here](https://www.auderer.at/en/).

Another delightful option is Hotel Stern, situated at Marktstraße 23, Imst, Austria. To book a stay or get more information, contact them at +43 5412 62305 or check out their website [here](https://www.stern-imst.at/).

Now let's move on to Landeck: Tyrolean Charm. Discover the essence of this charming place by staying at these remarkable hotels.

Experience warm hospitality at Hotel Schwarzer Adler on Malserstraße 31, Landeck, Austria. Contact them for reservations and inquiries at +43 5442 62532 or explore their website [here](https://www.schwarzer-adler.at/en/).

For a memorable stay in Landeck, consider Hotel Enzian located at Ing.-A.-Larcher-Straße 8. Reach out to them at +43 5442 62150 or visit their website [here](https://www.hotel-enzian.com/en/).

Next stop is Nauders: Alpine Adventure Hub. Unleash your adventurous spirit by staying in these fantastic hotels.

Hotel Post Nauders on Bundesstraße 197 offers an ideal base for your alpine adventures in Nauders. Contact them at +43 5473 87207 or visit their website [here](https://www.post-nauders.com/en/) for more details.

Indulge yourself with a stay at Hotel Berghof on Dorfstraße 32, Nauders, Austria. For reservations and inquiries, reach out to them at +43 5473 87100 or explore their website [here](https://www.hotel-berghof-nauders.com/en/).

Lastly, let's explore the Resia Pass to Merano: South Tyrolean Beauty. Immerse yourself in the breathtaking landscapes and stay at these exquisite hotels.

Experience true comfort at Hotel Margun located on Pinzonweg 42, Tirolo, Italy. Contact them at +39 0473 923520 or visit their website [here](https://www.margun.it/en/) for an unforgettable stay.

For a touch of elegance and luxury, consider Hotel Aurora situated on Freiheitsstrasse 45, Merano, Italy. Contact them at +39 0473 230333 or explore their website [here](https://www.aurora-meran.com/en/) to make your reservations.

When it comes to exploring the Via Claudia Augusta Radweg, having the right mobile navigation apps specifically designed for cyclists can greatly enhance your experience. These apps offer detailed maps, route guidance, and useful features tailored to the historic route. Here are some highly recommended mobile navigation apps that you should consider:

1. Komoot: Your Ultimate Outdoor Guide
   - Key Features:
     - Detailed maps exclusively for cycling routes.
     - Turn-by-turn voice navigation to keep you on track.
     - Elevation profiles and difficulty ratings for a challenging ride.
     - Offline maps for areas with limited connectivity.
     - Points of interest and highlights along the way to discover.
     - Community-driven content with valuable user recommendations.
   - Website and Download Link:
     - [Komoot](https://www.komoot.com/)
2. Strava: Track Your Ride
   - Key Features:
     - GPS tracking functionality for recording and sharing your rides.
     - Route planning using a vast global network of cycling routes.
     - Segments feature allows you to track and compete on specific sections.
     - In-depth analysis of ride data such as distance, speed, and elevation.
     - Community features that enable connections with fellow cyclists.
   - Website and Download Link:
     - [Strava](https://www.strava.com/)
3. Bikemap: Your All-in-One Cycling Map & GPS Navigation App
   - Key Features:
     - Comprehensive worldwide cycling route map at your fingertips.

- Turn-by-turn voice navigation ensures you stay on course effortlessly
- Offline maps available for uninterrupted exploration even without an internet connection
- Discover interesting points of interest along your journey
- Benefit from community-generated route recommendations
- Website and Download Link:
-[Bikemap](https://www.bikemap.net/)

4. Maps.me: Your Reliable Offline Maps & Navigation Companion
   - Key Features:
   - Access offline maps for seamless navigation without relying on an internet connection.
   - Detailed maps featuring cycling routes and notable landmarks.
   - Turn-by-turn navigation with clear voice guidance to keep you informed.
   - User-friendly interface makes route planning a breeze.
   - Convenient offline search functionality for locations and services.
   - Website and Download Link:
   - [Maps.me](https://maps.me/)

5. OsmAnd: Your Trusted Offline Maps, Travel, and Navigation App
   - Key Features:
   - Enjoy offline maps that provide detailed information about cycling routes.
   - Receive turn-by-turn voice guidance to stay on track effortlessly
   - Discover interesting points of interest and amenities along the way
   - Convenient offline search feature for finding locations and addresses
   - Utilize route planning and tracking features to optimize your journey
   - Website and Download Link:

-[OsmAnd](https://osmand.net/)
Before embarking on your cycling adventure along the Via Claudia Augusta Radweg, it is essential to download the necessary maps through these apps. Additionally, make sure to check for any available updates. Take some time to familiarize yourself with the features of these apps so that you can fully maximize your cycling experience. And always remember to prioritize safety while using navigation apps during your ride. Happy cycling!

When it comes to the Via Claudia Augusta Radweg, Local Tourist Information Centers play a crucial role in helping travelers. Their main goal is to enhance the cycling experience and ensure a smooth journey by providing valuable information, maps, and resources. Let's take a look at some key centers along the route:

1. Augsburg Tourist Information Center
   - Location: Rathausplatz 1, 86150 Augsburg, Germany
   - Contact Number: +49 821 5020700
   - Website: [Augsburg Tourist Information](https://www.augsburg-tourismus.de/)
2. Füssen Tourist Information
   - Location: Kaiser-Maximilian-Platz 1, 87629 Füssen, Germany
   - Contact Number: +49 8362 93850
   - Website: [Füssen Tourist Information](https://www.fuessen.de/)
3. Bolzano Tourist Board
   - Location: Piazza Walther, 8, 39100 Bolzano BZ, Italy
   - Contact Number: +39 0471 307000
   - Website: [Bolzano Tourism](https://www.bolzano-bozen.it/)
4. Trento Tourist Information Center
   - Location: Via Manci 2, 38122 Trento TN, Italy
   - Contact Number: +39 0461 216000
   - Website: [Visit Trentino](https://www.visittrentino.info/)
5. Verona Tourist Information
   - Location: Piazza Bra, 28, Verona VR., Italy
   - Contact Number:,+39 045 8068680
   - Website: [Verona Tourism](https://www.tourism.verona.it/)
6. Auer Tourist Information
   - Location: Rathausstraße 12, 39040 Auer BZ, Italy
   - Contact Number: +39 0471 810231
   - Website: [Auer Tourism](https://www.suedtirolerland.it/)
7. Trentino Marketing S.p.A.
   - Location: Via Romagnosi, 11, 38122 Trento TN, Italy
   - Contact Number: +39 0461 219500

  - Website: [Trentino
Marketing](https://www.visittrentino.info/)
  8. Donauwörth Tourist Information
    - Location: Rathausgasse 1, 86609 Donauwörth, Germany
    - Contact Number:,+49 906 7890
    - Website: [Donauwörth Tourist
Information](https://www.donauwoerth.de/)
  9. Landsberg am Lech Tourist Information
    - Location:,Hauptplatz 157,86899,Landsberg am Lech Germany
  - Telephone:+49-8191-320044
  - Website:[Landsberg am Lech
Tourism](https://www.landsberg.de/)
  10. Munich Tourist Information
    Location: Marienplatz 8,80331,München Germany
    Telephone:+49-89-23396500
    Website:[Munich Tourism](https://www.muenchen.de/)
These information centers offer a wide range of services to
cyclists traveling along the Via Claudia Augusta Radweg. Services
include maps for navigation purposes, suggestions for
accommodations, information about local highlights, and
assistance with any inquiries or questions cyclists may have during
their journey.

When it comes to cycling the Via Claudia Augusta Radweg, there are some additional tips that can greatly enhance your experience. These tips are designed to help you prepare for any situation and make the most of your journey. Let's dive into them:

1. Weather Readiness:

- Before you begin your adventure, it's important to check the weather forecast. The Alpine regions can be unpredictable, so make sure you have appropriate clothing and gear for any sudden changes.

2. Trail Etiquette:

- Show consideration for other cyclists and pedestrians by following trail etiquette. Keep to the right side, especially in narrow sections, and let others know when you're passing them.

3. Bike Maintenance:

- Ensure that your bike is in top condition before setting off on the route. Carry basic tools, a spare tube, and have some knowledge of how to handle minor repairs.

4. Staying Hydrated and Nourished:

- It's crucial to stay hydrated, particularly during warmer months. Bring a refillable water bottle with you and pack some snacks to keep your energy levels up. Take advantage of local cafes and restaurants along the way to savor regional cuisine.

5. Booking Accommodations in Advance:

- During peak seasons, it's wise to book accommodations ahead of time, especially in popular towns and cities along the route.

6. Navigation Apps or GPS Devices:

- Make use of mobile navigation apps or GPS devices specifically designed for cycling to ensure that you stay on track throughout your journey. Download offline maps in case you encounter areas with limited connectivity.

7. Emergency Preparedness:

- Save local emergency numbers and important contacts on your phone before starting your trip. Familiarize yourself with nearby hospitals or medical facilities along the route.

8. Respecting Local Customs:

- Show respect for the customs and traditions of the places you visit. Learn a few basic phrases in the local languages and be courteous to the locals you come across.

9. Proper Waste Disposal:

- Dispose of waste responsibly by carrying a small trash bag on your bike and using designated bins for litter.

10. Taking Rest and Recovery Seriously:

- Listen to your body and take breaks when necessary, especially during challenging sections. Plan rest days to explore interesting towns or attractions along the way.

11. Travel Insurance Coverage:

- It's important to have travel insurance that covers cycling activities. Check the coverage for medical emergencies, bike theft, or any unforeseen circumstances.

12. Embracing Cultural Events:

- Keep an eye on local event calendars for cultural festivals, markets, or special events happening along the route. Participating in these events can add memorable experiences to your journey.

13. Connecting with Fellow Cyclists:

- The Via Claudia Augusta Radweg is a popular cycling route, so there's a good chance you'll encounter other cyclists along the way. Connect with them, share experiences, and gather tips for your journey.

14. Capturing Memorable Moments:

- Don't forget to capture the scenic beauty of the route through photography. There will be plenty of opportunities to snap pictures of historic landmarks and breathtaking landscapes.

15. Being Aware of Trail Ratings:

- Take note of trail difficulty ratings for specific sections of the route. Adjust your pace and plan accordingly, especially if you're traveling with individuals who have varying skill levels.

By incorporating these additional tips into your Via Claudia Augusta Radweg adventure, you'll elevate your overall experience and ensure a truly memorable and enjoyable cycling journey through diverse landscapes and rich cultural heritage.